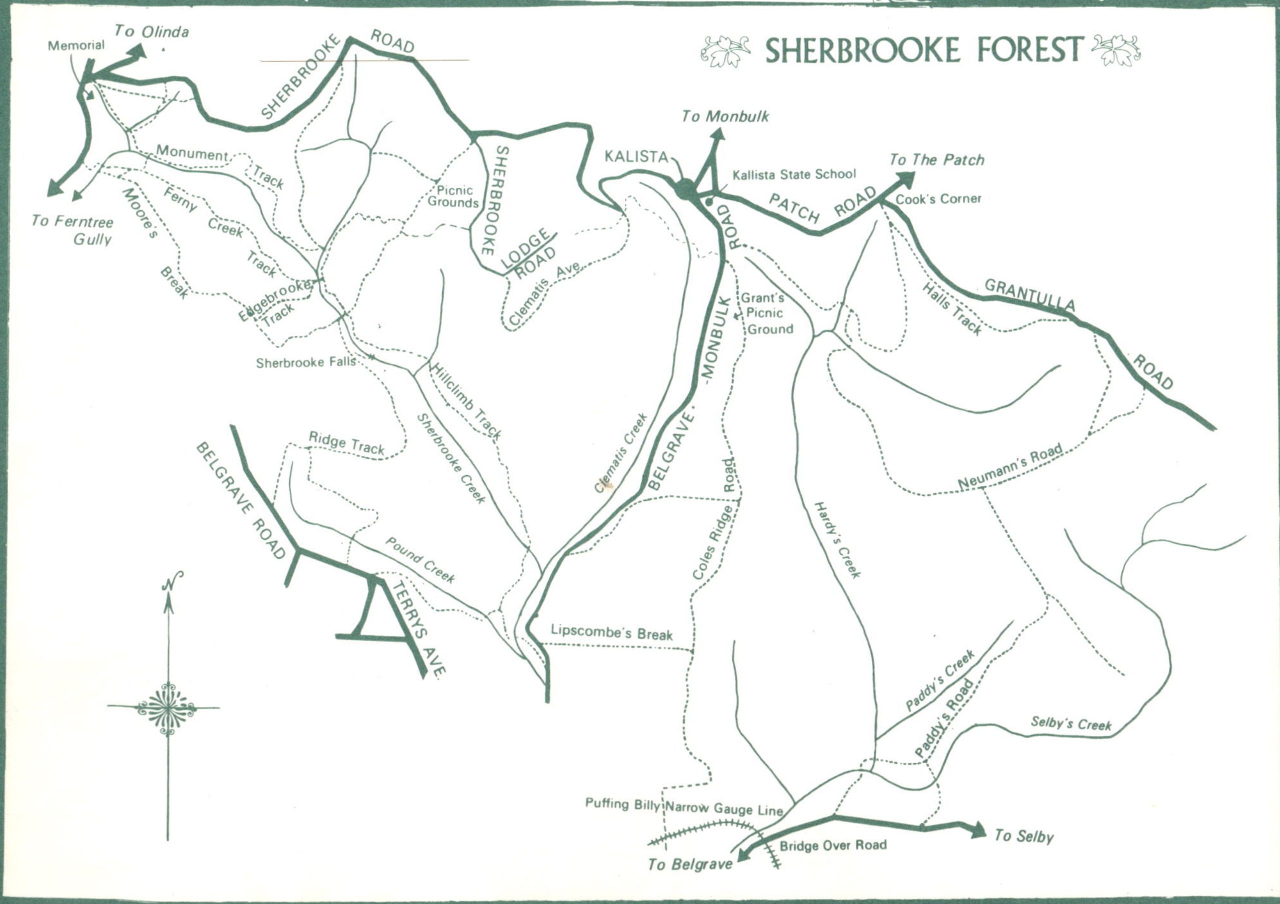

SHERBROOKE FOREST

To Olinda

Memorial

SHERBROOKE ROAD

Monument Track

SHERBROOKE LODGE ROAD

Picnic Grounds

Ferny Creek Track

Moore's Break

Eaglebrooke Track

Clematis Ave.

To Ferntree Gully

Sherbrooke Falls

Hillclimb Track

Ridge Track

Sherbrooke Creek

BELGRAVE ROAD

Pound Creek

TERRYS AVE.

Lipscombe's Break

Clematis Creek

BELGRAVE - MONBULK ROAD

Coles Ridge Road

KALISTA

To Monbulk

Kallista State School

PATCH ROAD

To The Patch

Cook's Corner

Grant's Picnic Ground

Halls Track

GRANTULLA ROAD

Neumann's Road

Hardy's Creek

Paddy's Creek

Paddy's Road

Selby's Creek

Puffing Billy Narrow Gauge Line

Bridge Over Road

To Belgrave

To Selby

N

THE DANDENONGS
IN COLOUR · RONALD RYAN
RIGBY

The Dandenongs in colour

In recent years, the "Blue Dandenongs"— twenty miles east of Melbourne—have become Victoria's major tourist attraction. Less than an hour's drive will take the visitor from the city into the heart of the ranges and tranquil surroundings, far removed from the bustle of the city.

From the foothill plains to the lookouts at over 2000 feet above sea level, there are magnificent views of the city, suburbs and Port Phillip Bay, the Mornington Peninsula and Western Port Bay to the south, and the Great Dividing Range and Mount Donna Buang to the north.

In the 1860s, only two generations ago, the first tentative steps towards the exploration of the Blue Hills to the east of Batman's village were taken by a handful of settlers with their flocks and herds. These pioneers were soon followed by woodsmen keen to begin a timber industry. When the gold began to play out at the Ballarat diggings, many disillusioned miners turned to the ranges as a possible new prospecting area. They followed the creeks in the hope of finding alluvial gold, and although gold proved elusive, the prospectors contributed significantly to the opening up of some of the more remote areas in the ranges.

Carl Nobelius, a Swedish nurseryman, recognised the potential of the rich red soil and established an extensive nursery of fruit and ornamental trees at Emerald. As a direct result of Nobelius' success with this project, a land boom began. Large numbers of families moved into the area and took up small holdings, which they planted with a variety of crops. This pattern of moderate-scale, mixed farming by family groups is still evident today.

In the north and in the foothills to the south-west, the residents are mainly concerned with dairy farming, fruit growing, jam making and nursery farming. Apart from tropical varieties, virtually every type of fruit and vegetable is grown in the Dandenongs. "The market gardens of Melbourne" would be an accurate description of the area. In the richer, red-black, acidic soils, intensive cultivation achieves maximum productivity for those who are prepared to work hard and for long hours. The ranges are a melting pot of nationalities, with Dutch and Yugoslavs, Irish and Hungarians, Italians and descendants of the original settlers working hard and in harmony on adjoining blocks.

The entire region abounds with wildlife, much of which is rigorously protected. At various times during the year, the forests come alive with the songs of common and rare birds—the crisp, clear call of the bellbird, the incessant chatter of the kookaburra, the amazing mimicry of the lyrebird and busy noises of roving flocks of colourful rosellas. For the enthusiast, there is always the challenge of seeking out the rare, almost extinct Helmeted Honeyeater.

No matter what the season, "The Hills" seem to have some outstanding attraction to interest the visitor. The ranges seem to amplify the characteristics of the seasons. In autumn, the burnt oranges, yellows and auburns of the imported and native shrubs and trees are juxtaposed against the evergreen eucalypts. An occasional sprinkling of snow falls on Mount Dandenong and around Olinda in winter, and at this time of the year, the lyrebirds begin their elaborate courtship rituals in Sherbrooke Forest. Spring brings floral festivals, such as the National Rhododendron Society's annual display of which the Tecoma Floral Carpet is a feature. Not to be missed is the Silvan South Tulip Farm's dazzling display which lasts only from 21 September to 10 October. A month later, the Lilium Shows add further colour to the area.

A year-round feature of the hills is the great range of international restaurants covering the area. Most of the outstanding eating places adopt a national theme, accurately detailing the architecture, decor and cuisine of that country. Some of the most well-known are the Zuider Zee, the Peppercorn, Coonara Springs, the Cuckoo, Kenloch and Fiddler's Green near Olinda, the Blue Peacock at Monbulk, Tatra Hut and Skyhigh Restaurant at Mount Dandenong, the Red Mill and Highwood at Belgrave, Hunter's Lodge and Dorset Gardens in the foothills near Croydon, Chateau Wyuna north of Montrose and Sherbrooke Lodge at Sherbrooke.

The intimate live theatres of the Basin Theatre Group and the 1812 Theatre at Lysterfield consistently attract full houses. Both groups will soon move into newly-designed theatres.

The Olinda Falls, easily accessible from Falls Road, provide an idyllic setting among graceful tree-ferns for the whiling away of a few weekend hours. Sherbrooke Falls, only half a mile from

Sherbrooke Lodge Road, easily warrants the walk through the bush from the road.

In the central ranges lie large areas of National Parkland. Majestic Mountain Ash trees grow beside mixed species of Eucalypts in Sherbrooke Forest, Ferntree Gully National Park and the Olinda forest. The yearly rainfall of fifty-six inches produces a dense growth of tree-ferns and a ground cover of smaller ferns and fungi, contrasting with the spiralling effect of the straight, tall trees. Myriads of interconnecting pathways provide the walker with delights, such as the arrival of a lyrebird in his path, scratching around apparently unconcerned, but ever-alert for signs of danger. At the slightest disturbance, the lyrebird will melt away into the bush.

Contrasting with the random beauty of the National Parks are the carefully landscaped gardens of the Doongalla Estate at The Basin and the Alfred Nicholas Memorial Gardens at Sherbrooke. Both can be inspected by the public.

Adjoining the National Parks, the Silvan Reserve and Emerald Lake provide ideal venues for group outings during the hotter months. The mystical characters of Aboriginal legend depicted in carvings at the William Ricketts Sanctuary at Mount Dandenong hold a fascination for both local and overseas visitors. Perhaps the greatest of all the Dandenongs' attractions, particularly for the young, is the trip on "Puffing Billy," the only narrow-gauge train of its kind in Australia still operating in its original condition.

Some of the residents of the ranges, particularly in the area from Ferntree Gully to Belgrave, now think of their region as part of Melbourne's mushrooming suburbia. Despite the travelling time to the city, many residents have chosen to live in the ranges and commute daily to their jobs in the city. Their homes, blending so well with the surrounding landscape, give relief and contentment to the city worker prepared to make the trip to the metropolis and back each day.

Fine stands of Mountain Ash, such as this one in Sherbrooke Forest, grow to over three hundred feet. Misty mornings provide ideal conditions for observation of the many lyrebirds in this forest.

Aerial view of city of Melbourne (on left) and suburbs, with the Dandenong Ranges in the background. The Yarra River appears in the centre, with the uncompleted Westgate Bridge in the foreground.

Traditional green-roofed homestead, surrounded by the brilliant autumn colours of the Silver Birch, provides a contrast against the evergreen eucalypts.

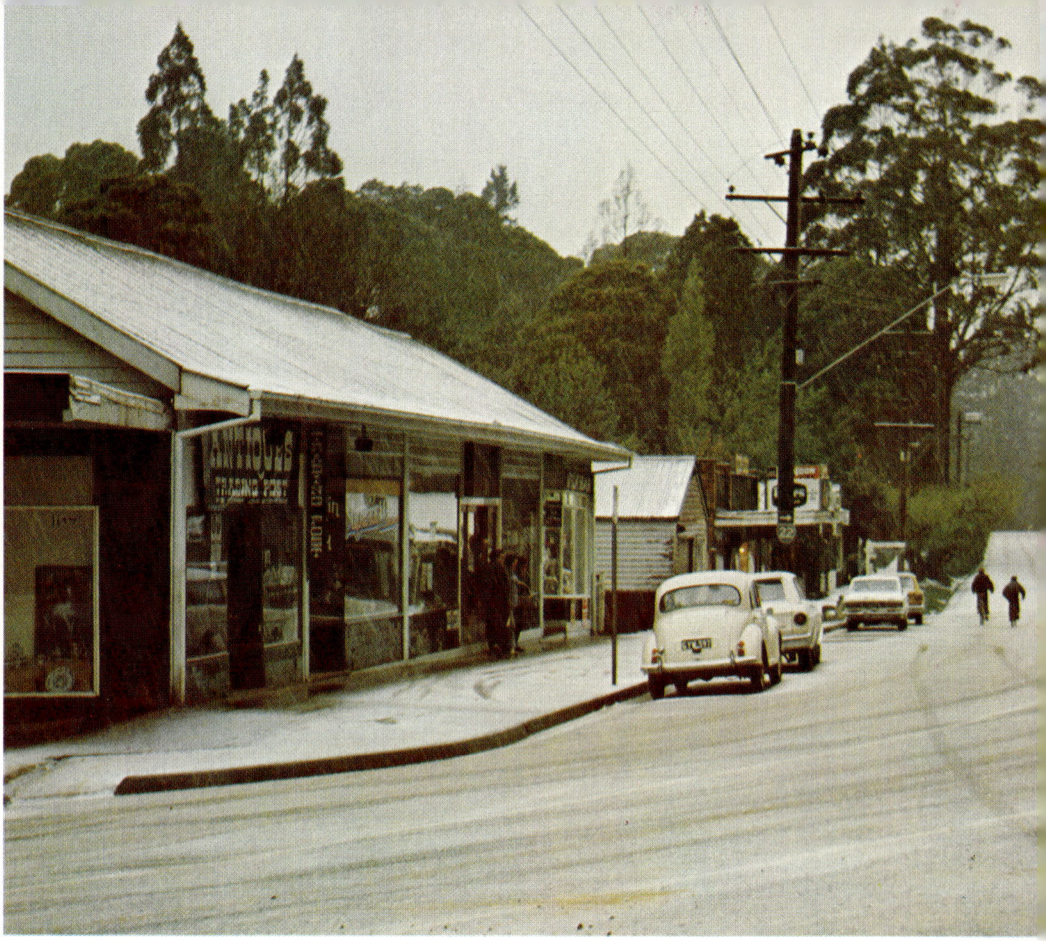
ANTIQUES
TRADING POST

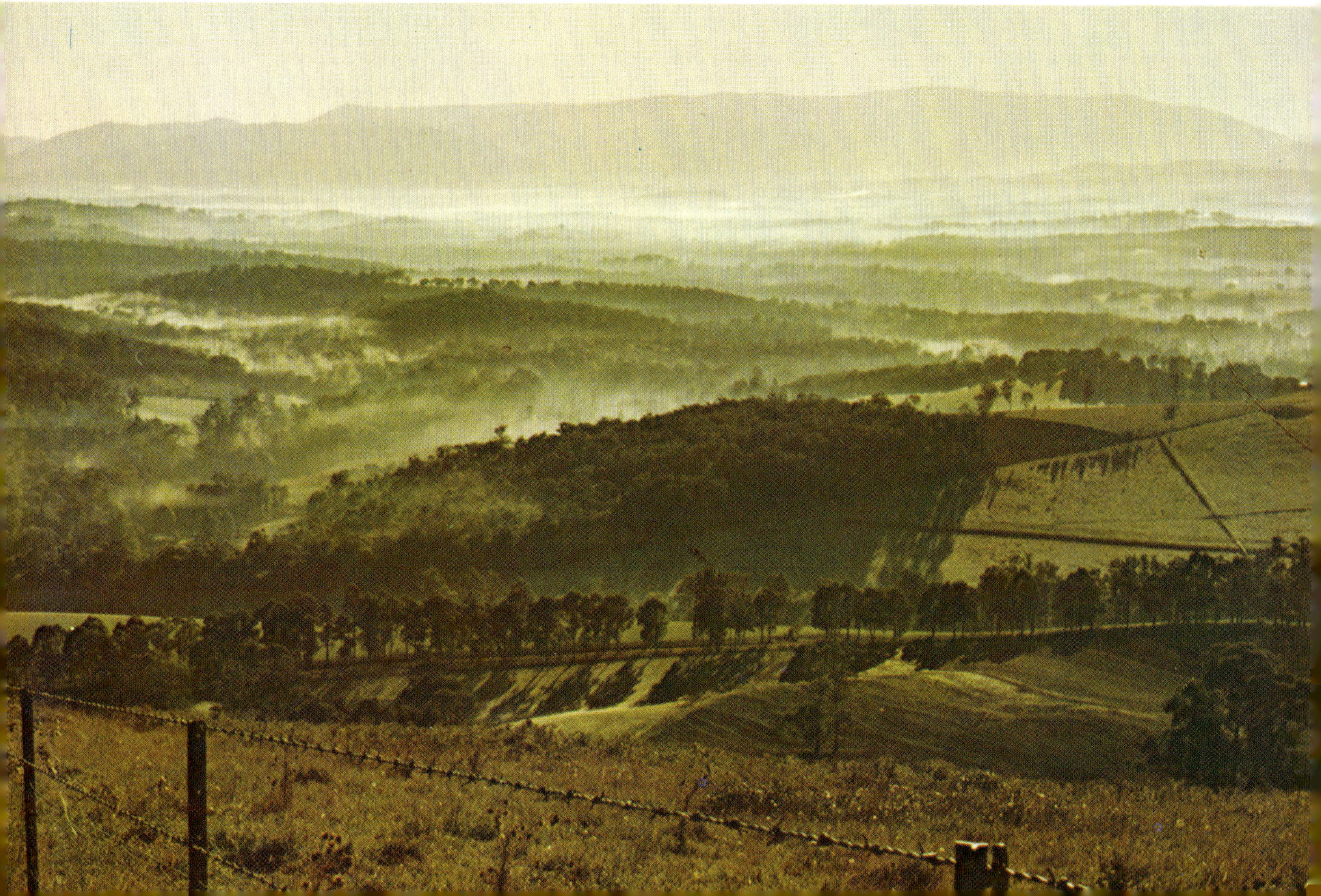

Left: Light snow falling
in Main Street, Olinda.

Below: From this point on Ridge Road near The Patch,
the visitor is treated to panoramic views across rolling
hills towards Donna Buang on one side, and over the
Cardinia Creek Reserve towards the ocean on the other.

Above: Random patches of flowers grow in the Dandenongs where seeds from nearby nurseries have been dispersed by winds. Mount Donna Buang is seen in the background.

Above: The lush green of these pastures near Grantulla Road, Menzies Creek, merge into the bush of Sherbrooke Forest Park and then into the blue haze over the hills in the background.

Opposite: Fog laying in the gullies of farm land around Cockatoo.

Above: An example of the diversity of farming is the breeding of goats at Wandin East, for their milk.

Left: Hyacinth-orchids form a brilliant border to the drive of this Monbulk nursery, typical of many which operate throughout this area.

Right: Dairy farms around Macclesfield supply fresh milk to the heavily-populated areas of Ferntree Gully, Upwey, Tecoma, and Belgrave.

The heavy rainfall in the Sherbrooke Forest region
encourages profuse growth of large tree ferns and a
wide variety of fungi and mosses.

Above: A unique photo of a mature male Superb Lyrebird (at right) teaching a younger bird, possibly one of his offspring, to dance on the mound. The two birds hop from one leg to another, and move in full circles around the mound with a continual "click-click." When the female is coaxed on to the mound, she will dance in the same manner, touching beaks with the male.

Right: During early winter, the male will clear a small patch in the forest removing all ferns. He will then raise the centre to about a foot above the surrounding area. He may clear as many as eight mounds which will act as the boundaries of his territory. The position of the lyrebird's tail may change many times during the display. The body will be completely obscured (as in this photo) or the lyrates (outside feathers) may take on the shape of a lyre.

Right: Golden autumn leaves throughout the hills impress visitors, but they are a problem to the residents once the trees begin shedding their leaves. Tunnels of smoke can be seen rising out of the forest, eventually leaving a smoky blue cast over the whole mountain range.

Below: Heavy frosts around Emerald cause the colours of autumn to last until early winter. The hills are considered by many to be at their peak of beauty during autumn.

Above: Riding schools, such as this one at Lysterfield, enable casual riders to see the foothills on horseback. The riders can enjoy the day with friends or join one of the organised parties.

Left: The Kallista Art Group gives aspiring painters in the area a chance to show their works to the public. The group holds regular exhibitions at different locations around the hills.

Right: Silvan Reservoir, opened in 1931, has long been a popular site for picnickers and social group outings. It is open throughout the year during daylight hours.

Above: The Baron of Beef reflects the opulence of a gracious period in English history. The Dandenongs are renowned for its many restaurants of international standards and cuisine.

Right: Guests arriving at the Baron of Beef Restaurant in Sherbrooke are greeted by a doorman dressed as an authentic English Beefeater.

Above: Built in 1928, the gracious Emerald Country Club is set in two hundred acres of beautifully maintained grounds. The club caters for its members with such varied activities as golf, tennis, croquet, bowls, and swimming— as well as having fine residential facilities.

Left: The William Ricketts Sanctuary at Mount Dandenong offers the unique spectacle of a visionary man's work in a natural forest setting. The Sanctuary, enlarged to fourteen acres and administered by the Victorian Forest Commission, attracts thousands of visitors from all over the world. Hundreds of sculptured works on the theme of Aboriginal mythology, wildlife, and conservation are set among streams, waterfalls, ferns, and natural bushland.

Due to be completed in June 1973, the Cardinia Creek Reservoir will supplement Melbourne's water supply. The Western Diversion Dam will provide facilities for light boating and water sports. The extensive landscape gardening on the reserve, with its planned amenities will prove to be popular for family outings.

Above: Puffing Billy shortly after leaving Belgrave.

The diminutive Puffing Billy engines pull carriage loads of children along the seven mile narrow-gauge track between Belgrave and Emerald three times a day on weekends and public holidays. A short stop at the Menzies Creek Puffing Billy Museum gives the engine crew a chance to take on water for the last few miles of the trip into Emerald. Restoration of an extended section of the track will soon take the train on to nearby Emerald Lake.

Above: The raucous laughter of the
kookaburra is a familiar sound and the
audacious birds have been known to fly
off with meat being barbecued by
picnickers.

Right: Only one colony of the Helmeted
Honey-eater now exists in Victoria, this
being at the State Wild Life Sanctuary at
Yellingbo. This bird was last year gazetted
as the State's Faunal Emblem. Its
sensitivity to intrusion on its environment
is threatening its existence as a species.

Above: Until recently, Albert Kent worked what is Victoria's only remaining bullock team, hauling logs through the dense bush at Mount Dandenong.

Left: The coarse bark is stripped from the trunk so that the logs will slide more easily to the loading ramp.

Right: One of the highlights of the year is the tulip season at Tesselaar's Tulip Farm in Main Road, Silvan. Blooms of extraordinary colour are in full flower from 25 September to 10 October.

The erect plant of the Common Heath, with its small
white, pink, or rose bells, grows in profusion
throughout the hills. It has been chosen as Victoria's
Floral Emblem.

Above: The Bottle-Brush is restricted to the more sandy soil in the south around Lysterfield Reservoir and Narre Warren North.

Right: The vivid flower of the Scarlet Flowering Gum contrasts with the evergreen eucalypt leaves.

Above: White Watsonia, flowering early in summer, frames a scene of a farmer hard at work turning the soil in readiness for his next crop.

Left: Another native flower growing in the Dandenongs is the Hill or Hairpin Banksia, which can be distinguished by its "hairpin" shaped styles. Flowering in winter, the honey-coloured brushes grow to a height of ten inches.

Right: Many varieties of gladioli are growing at Major Money's farm near Mount Evelyn. Blooms of all colours are on display from April to December.

Below: Begonias being planted by this Italian family will soon provide another colour in the floral patchwork of the Dandenongs.

Above: Young scouts have a meal before setting out on a trek through Ferntree Gully National Park to One Tree Hill lookout tower.

Left: The beauty of autumn is clearly shown in the brilliance of the many ornamental trees which are scattered throughout the hills.

Right: The potato harvest spans twelve months and is a source of employment for many students during vacation.

Below: The age-old process of jam-making has remained constant over the years. Plums from nearby orchards provide an immediate supply of fresh fruit, which is made into jam at the peak of its goodness.

Above: This ornamental lake is the focal point of a system of paths and walk-ways in the Alfred Nicholas Memorial Gardens in Sherbrooke Road, Sherbrooke. The gardens were formerly part of the Burnham Beeches Estate owned by the Nicholas drug-manufacturing family. They were handed over to Sherbrooke Shire in 1965, but became overgrown. They are now leased by Horst Koslowski and Alex Robson, who are restoring them to their former beauty.

Left: Hydrangeas and montbretias grow freely along the roadside particularly in the vicinity of Ferny Creek.

Intensive farming on small holdings provide a
sequence of year-round growing and harvesting of
a variety of crops, such as potatoes, strawberries,
carrots, and fruit trees.

Nestling amid tree ferns and eucalypts, houses like this at Belgrave illustrate their owner's desire to live in harmony with the bush.

RIGBY LIMITED • ADELAIDE • SYDNEY • MELBOURNE • BRISBANE • PERTH

First published 1973
Copyright © 1973 Ronald Ryan
Library of Congress Catalog Card Number 73-75267
National Library of Australia Registry Card
Number and ISBN 0 85179 559 5

Wholly designed and set up in Australia
Printed in Hong Kong